THE BOY'S CHANGING VOICE

20 VOCAL SOLOS

COMPILED AND EDITED BY
RICHARD WALTERS

To access companion recorded accompaniments online, visit:
www.halleonard.com/mylibrary

Enter Code
5083-0947-8557-7037

CONTENTS

PIANIST ON THE RECORDINGS:
Laura Ward

The price of this publication includes access to companion recorded accompaniments online, for download or streaming, using the unique code found on the title page. Visit **www.halleonard.com/mylibrary** and enter to access code.

Aura Lee

W.W. Fosdick
(1825–1862)

George R. Poulton
(1828–1867)

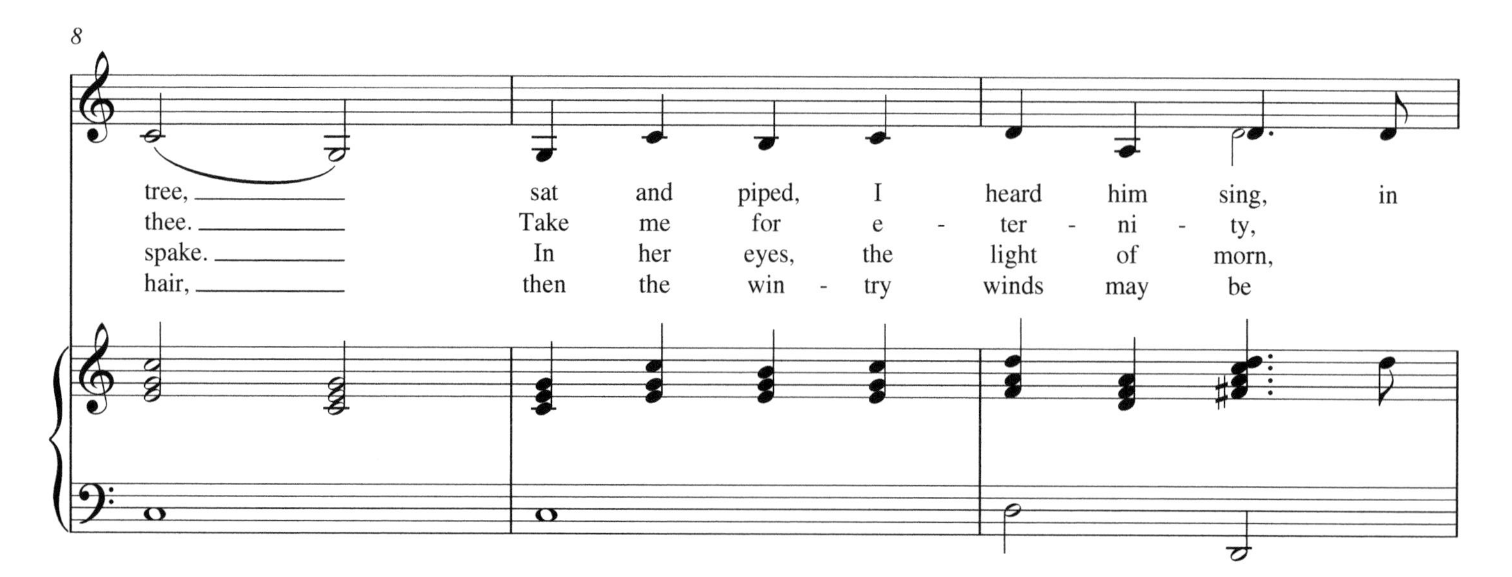

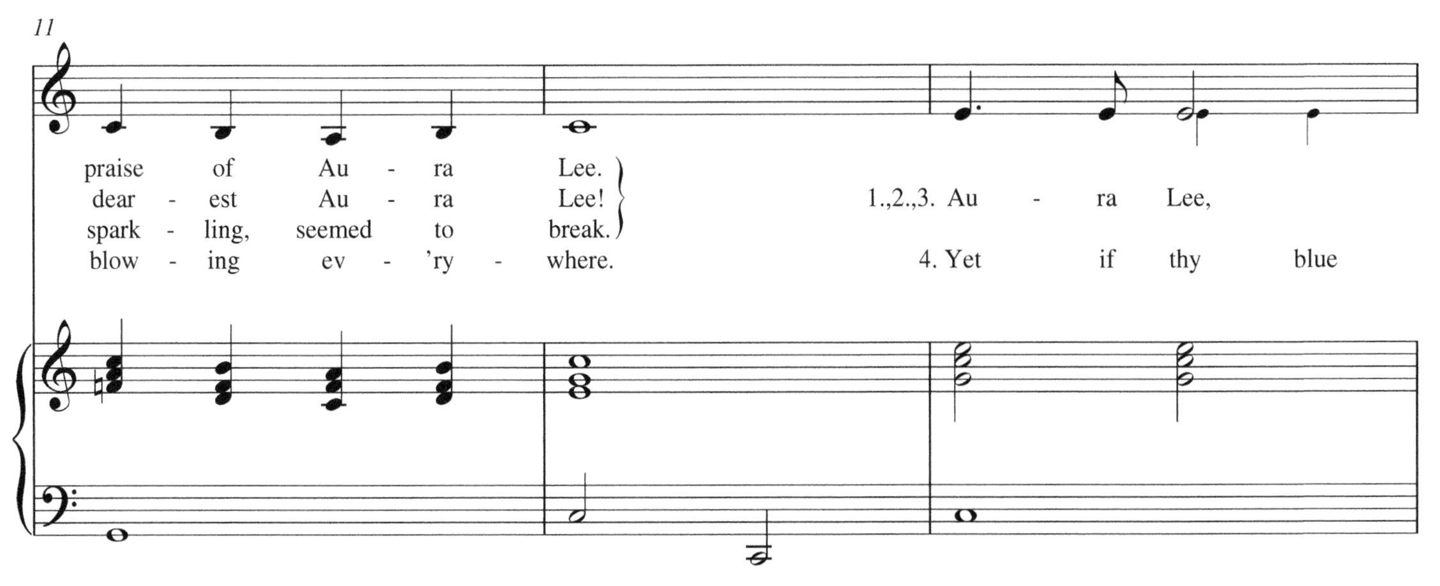
11
praise of Au - ra Lee.
dear - est Au - ra Lee!
spark - ling, seemed to break.
blow - ing ev - 'ry - where.
1.,2.,3. Au - ra Lee,
4. Yet if thy blue

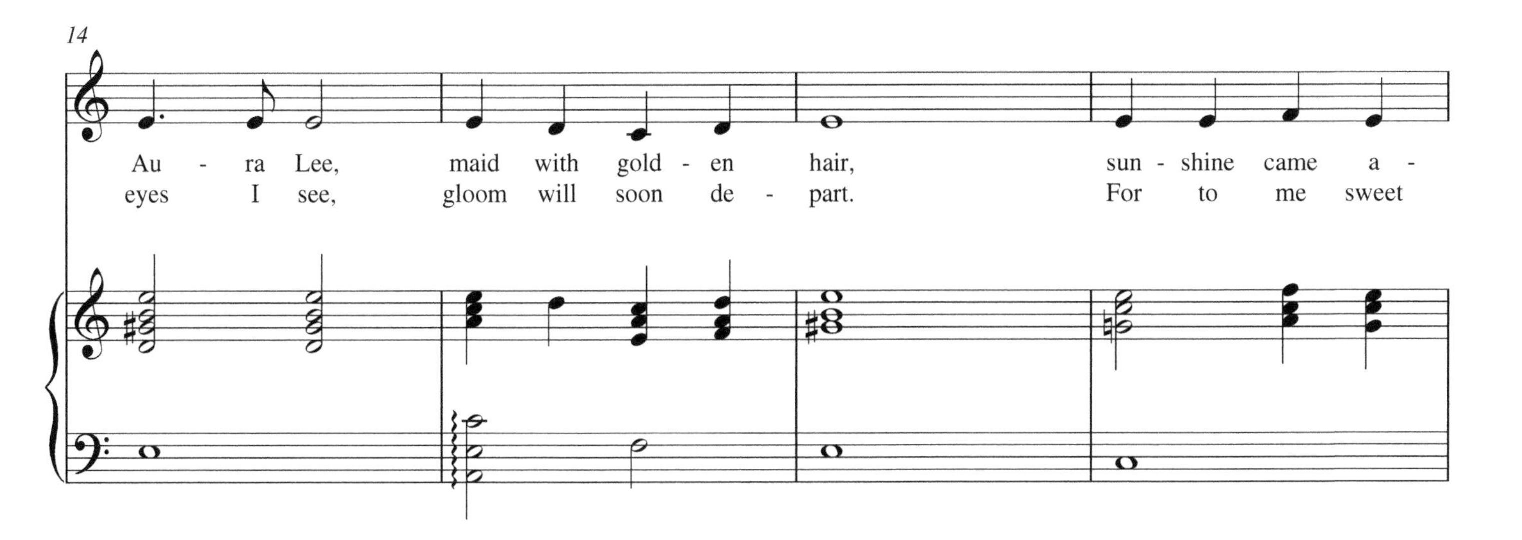
14
Au - ra Lee, maid with gold - en hair, sun - shine came a -
eyes I see, gloom will soon de - part. For to me sweet

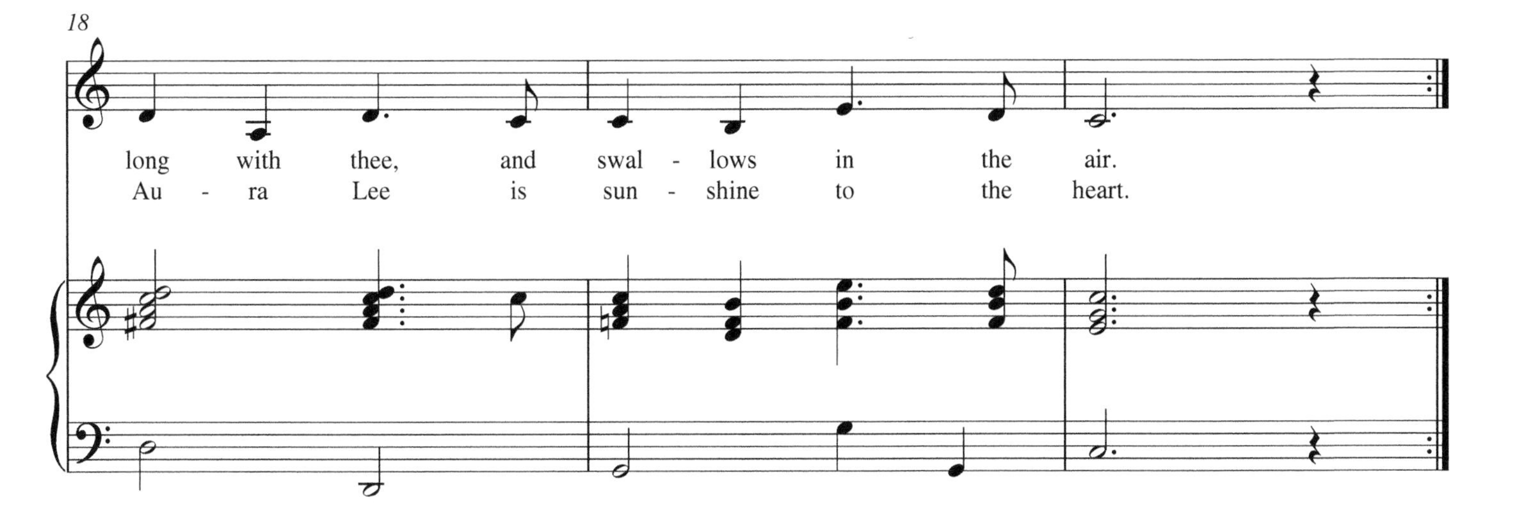
18
long with thee, and swal - lows in the air.
Au - ra Lee is sun - shine to the heart.

Barbara Allen

Scottish Folksong
arranged by Bryan Stanley

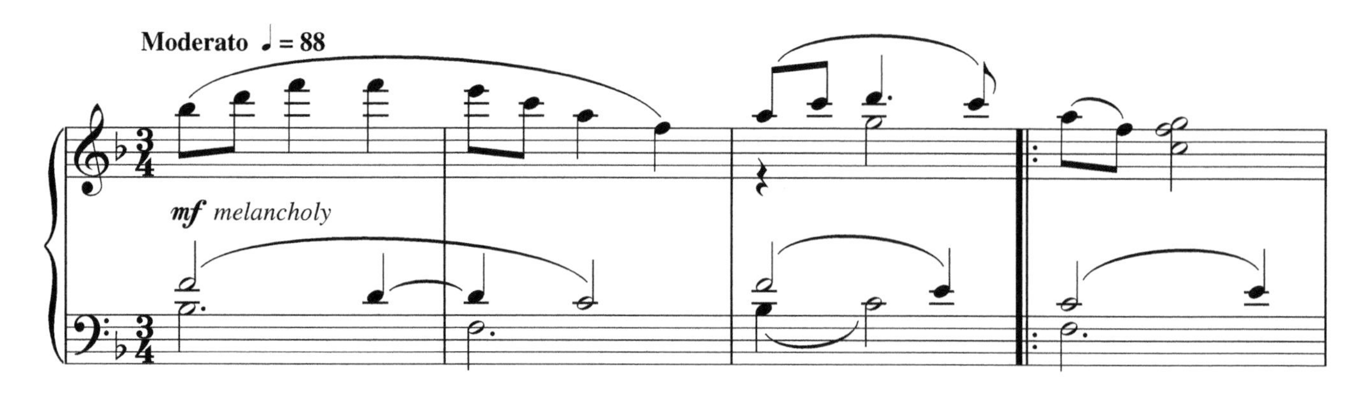

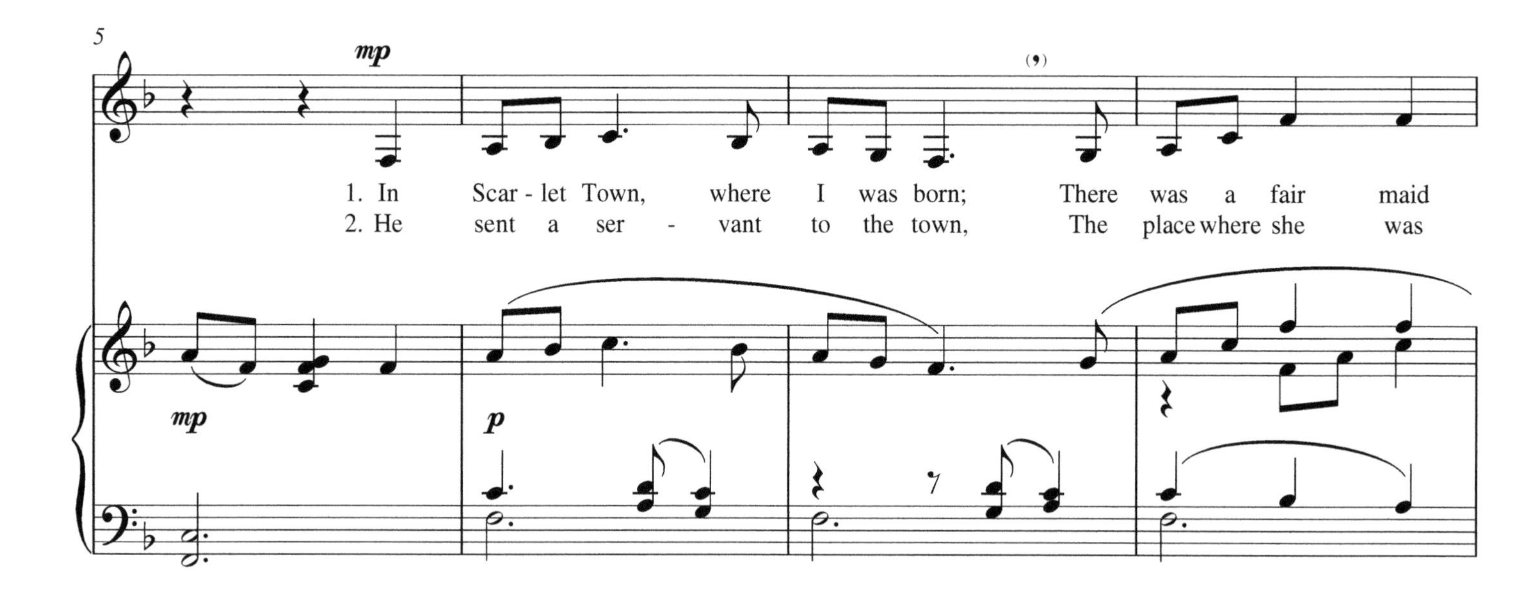

13
Al - len. 'Twas in the mer - ry month of May, When green buds they were
Al - len." And as she crossed the wood - ed fields, She heard his death - bell
17
swell - in'. Sweet Wil - liam on his death - bed lay for love of Bar - b'ra
knell - in', And ev - 'ry stroke, it spoke her name, "Hard - heart - ed Bar - b'ra
21
Al - len.
Al - len."
3. O Moth - er, Moth - er,
26
make my bed, And make it long and nar - row. Sweet Wil - liam died for

30
(𝄒)
’
love of me; I’ll die for him of sor - row.” “Fare - well,” she said, “ye

34
(𝄒)
’
maid - ens all, And shun the fault I fell in: Hence - forth take warn - ing

38
(𝄒)
by the fall Of cru - el Bar - b’ra Al - len,
mf

42
rit.
cru - el Bar - b’ra Al - len.”
rit.
p

All Through the Night

Welsh Folksong
arranged by Nicholl

Bendemeer's Stream

Thomas Moore
(1779–1852)

Traditional Irish Folk Melody

19
hear the bird's song. That bow'r and its mu - sic I nev - er for -
sum - mer was gone; Thus mem - o - ry draws from de - light e'er it

24
get, But oft when a - lone in the bloom of the year, I
dies An es - sence that breathes of it man - y a year; Thus

29
think, "Is the night - in - gale sing - ing there yet? Are the ros - es still
bright to my soul as 'twas then to my eyes, Is that bow'r on the
34
1
2
bright by the calm Ben - de - meer?" 2. No the
banks of the calm Ben - de - meer!

Bill Groggin's Goat

Southern Appalachian Folksong
arranged by Richard Walters

10
goat, in - deed he did,

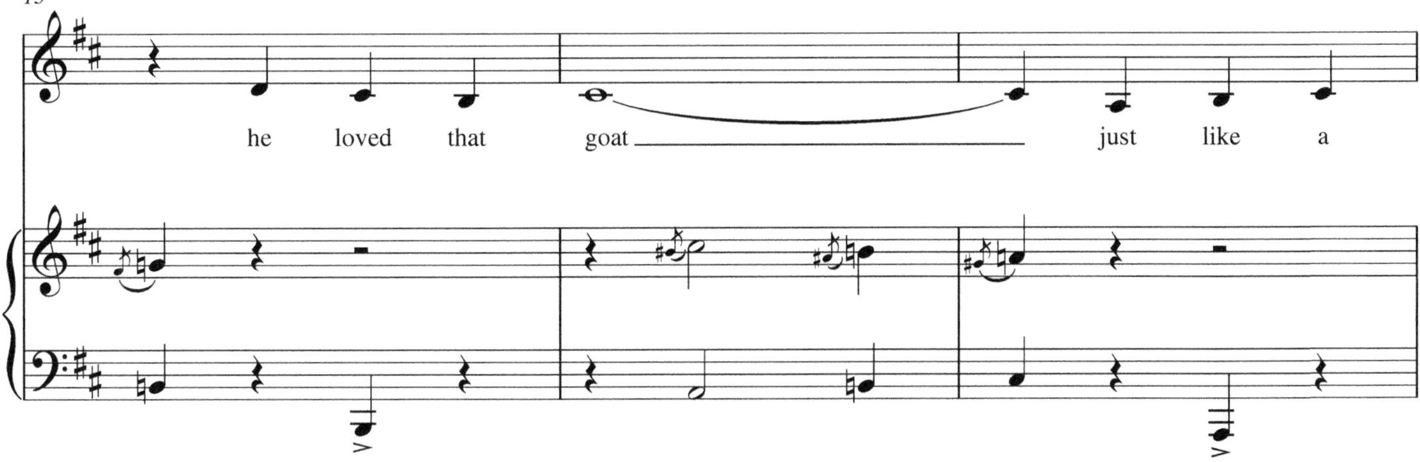
13
he loved that goat just like a

16
kid.
2. One day the

20
goat felt frisk and fine,
ate three red

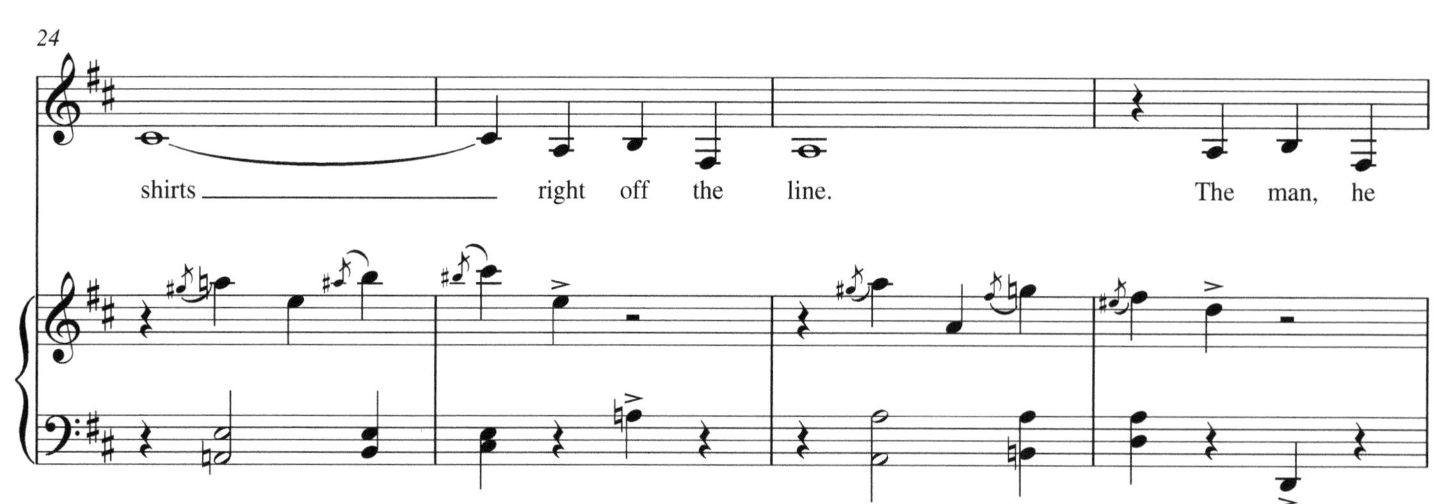
24
shirts right off the line. The man, he

28
grabbed him by the back and tied him

32
to a rail - road track.

36
3. Now, when the train came in - to
f

40
sight, that goat grew pale and green with

44
opt.
fright. He heaved a sigh as if in

48
pain, coughed up those shirts

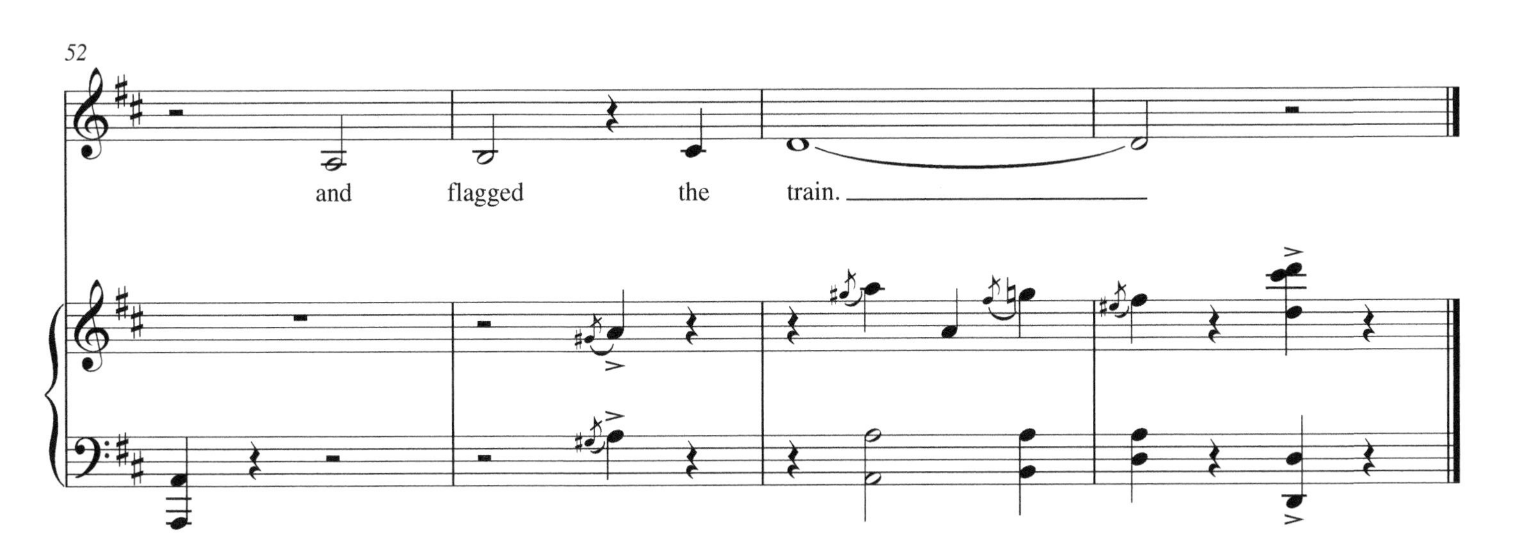
52
and flagged the train.

Bury Me Not on the Lone Prairie

Rev. Edwin H. Chapin
(1814–1880)

Cowboy Ballad, 1870s
Attributed to H. Clemens of South Dakota
Music by Ossian N. Dodge
(1820–1876)

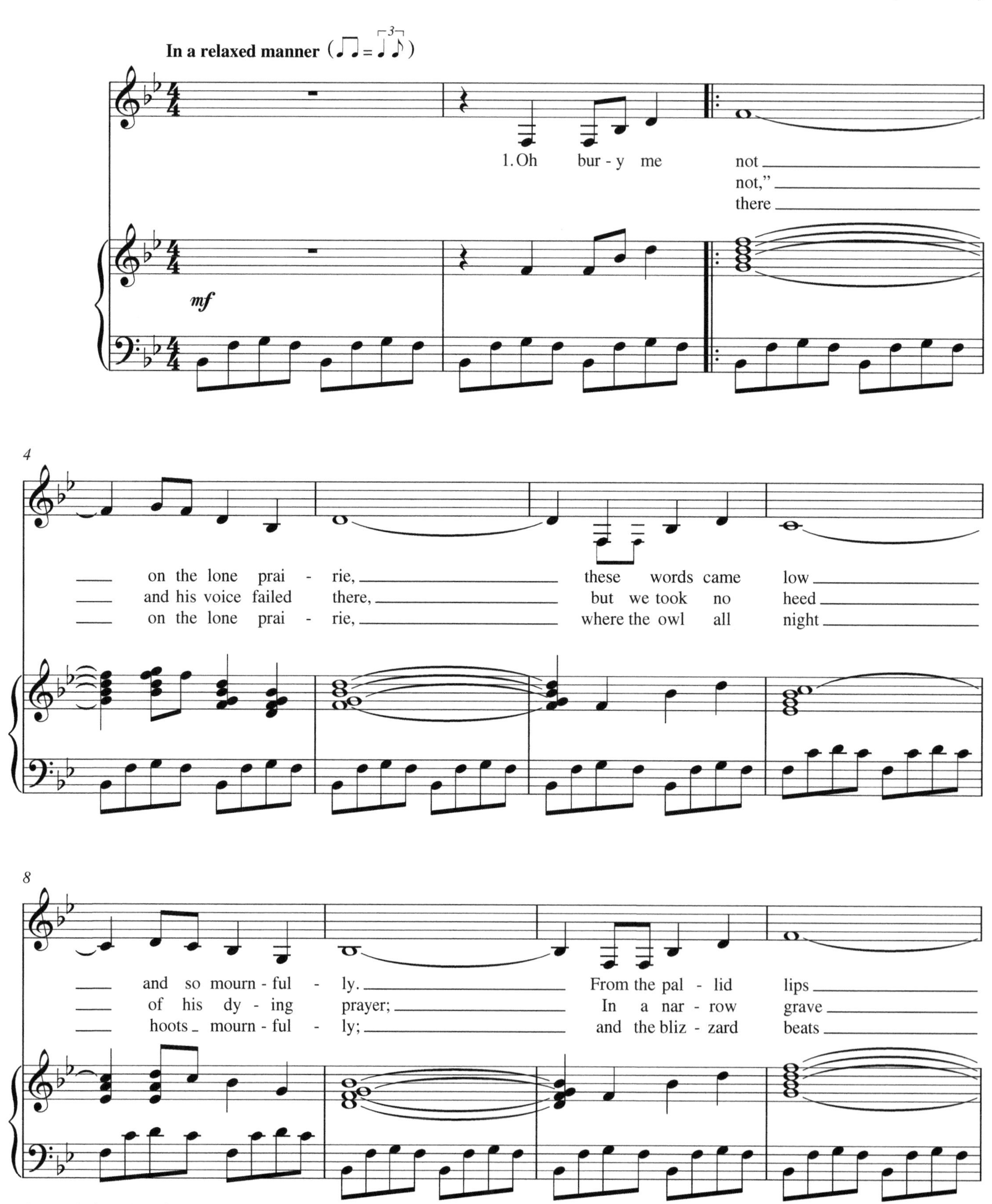

A parody based on the 1849 song "The Ocean Burial"

12
of a youth who lay, on his dy - ing
just six by three, we bur - ied him
and the wind blows free o'er his lone - ly
15
1, 2
bed at the close of day. 2. "Oh bur - y me
there on the lone prai - rie. 3. Yes, we bur - ied him
grave on the lone prai - rie,

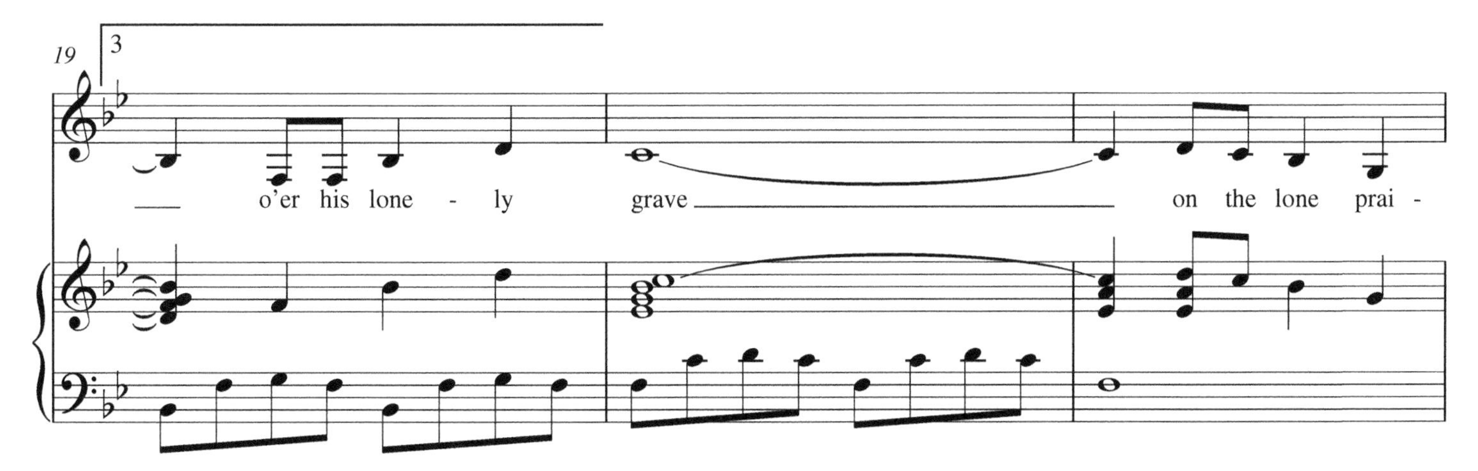
19
3
o'er his lone - ly grave on the lone prai -

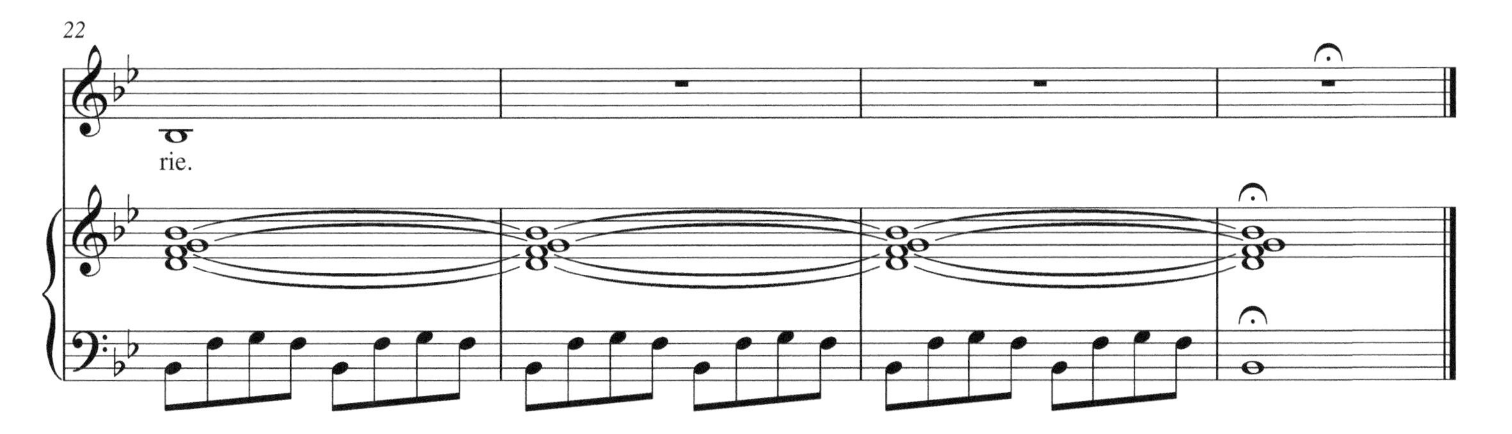
22
rie.

Come again, sweet love

Anonymous

John Dowland
(1563–1626)
realized by Richard Walters

*Small size notes are optional for verse two.

11
cresc.
decresc.
to die with thee a - gain in
I die in dead - ly pain and
mf
decresc.

14
p
sweet - est sym - pa - thy. To see, to hear,
end - less mis - er - y. I sit, I sigh,
p

17
cresc.
to touch, to kiss, to die
I weep, I faint, I die
mf

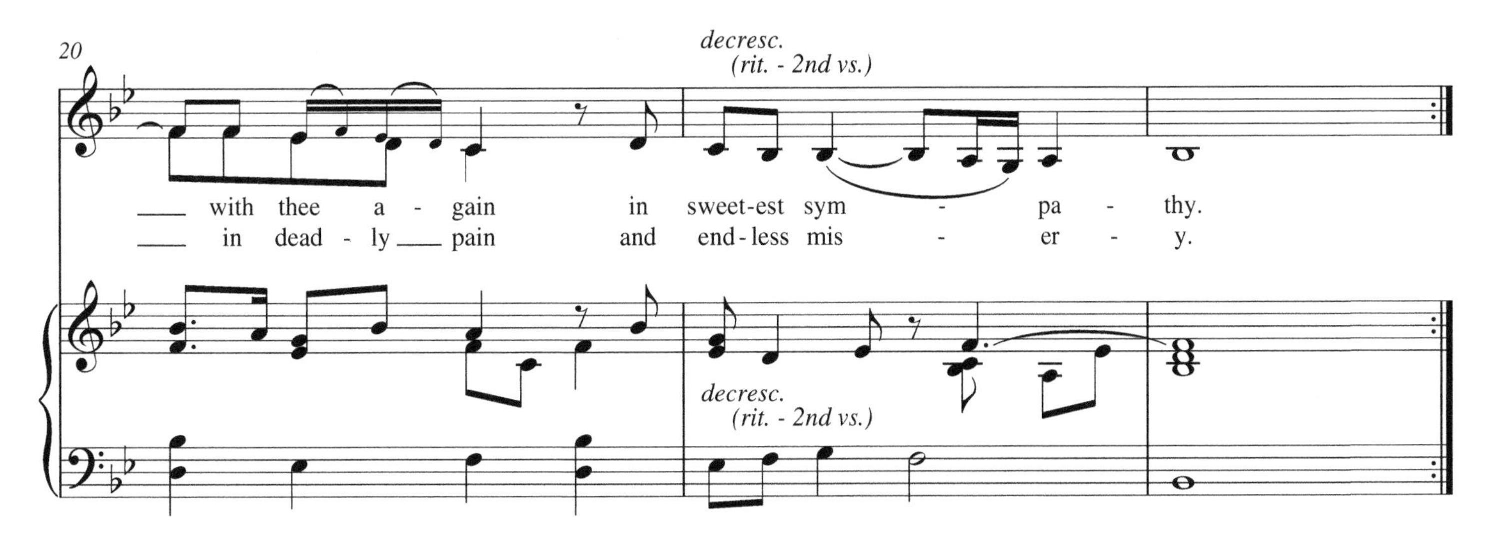
20
decresc.
(rit. - 2nd vs.)
with thee a - gain in sweet-est sym - pa - thy.
in dead - ly pain and end - less mis - er - y.
decresc.
(rit. - 2nd vs.)

Drink to Me Only with Thine Eyes

Ben Jonson
(1572–1637)

Music based on an English Folksong
arranged by Brian Dean

cresc.
I'll not look for wine. The

thirst that from the soul doth rise Doth
mp
mf

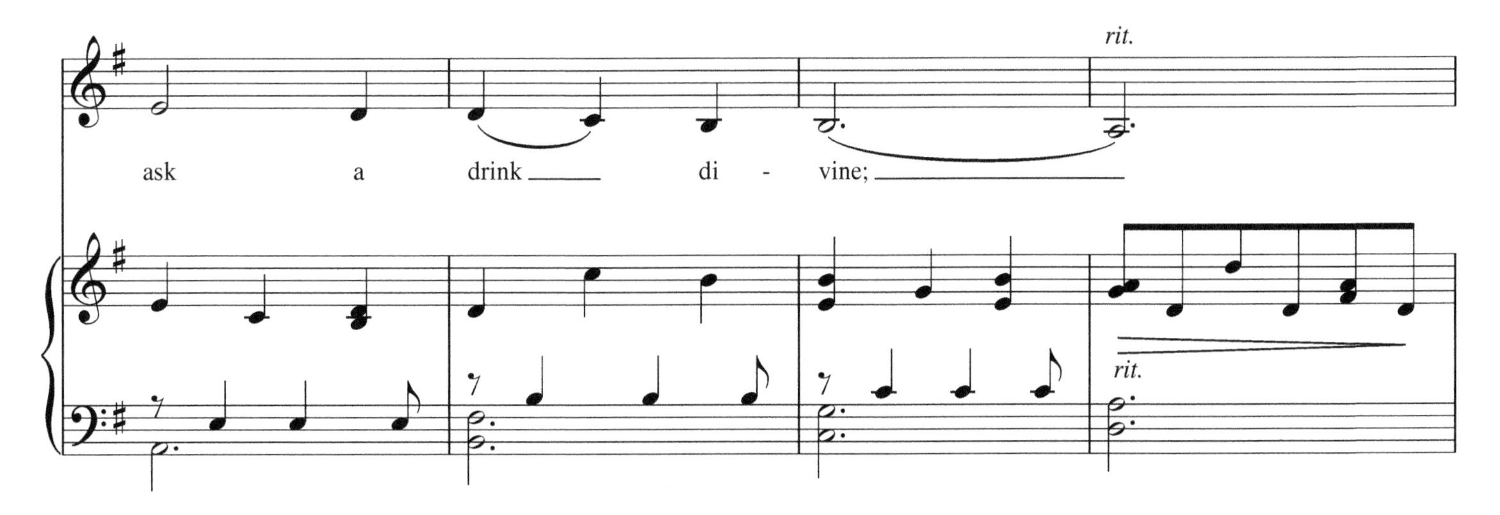
rit.
ask a drink di - vine;
rit.

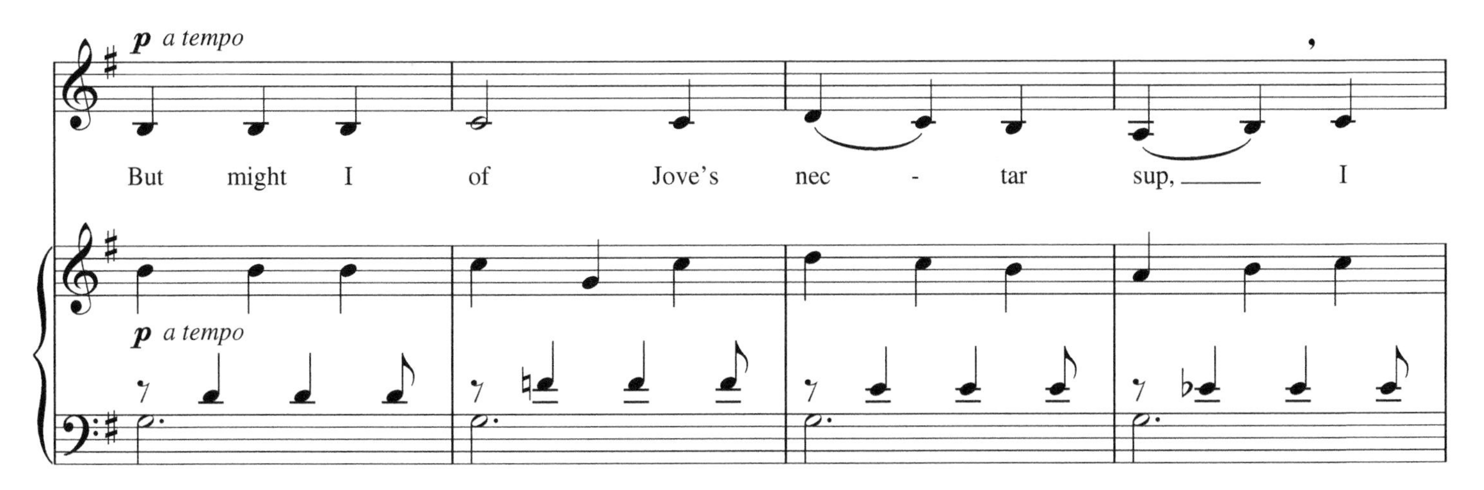
p a tempo
But might I of Jove's nec - tar sup, I
p a tempo

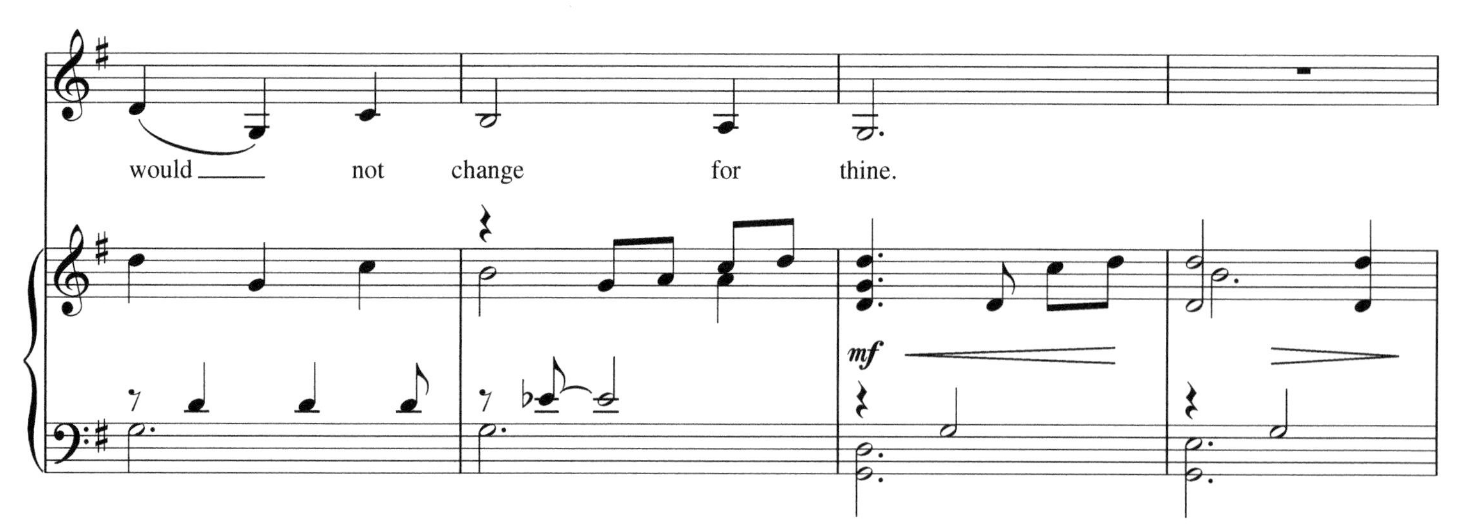
would not change for thine.
mf

mp
2. I sent thee late a
mp

ro - sy wreath, Not so much hon - 'ring

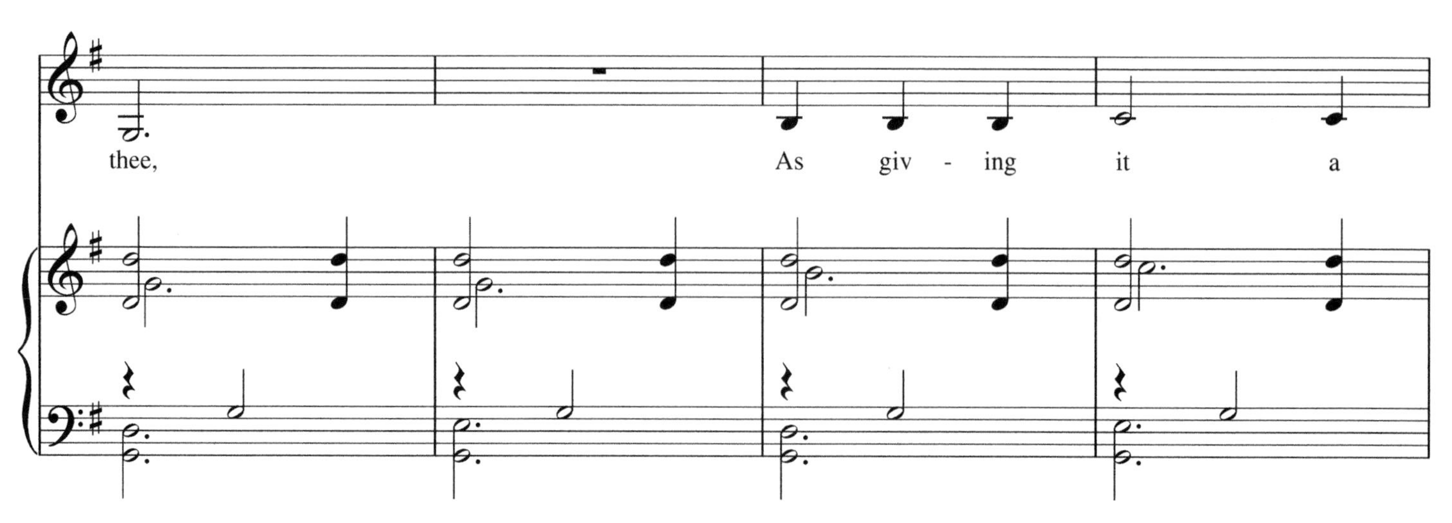
thee, As giv - ing it a

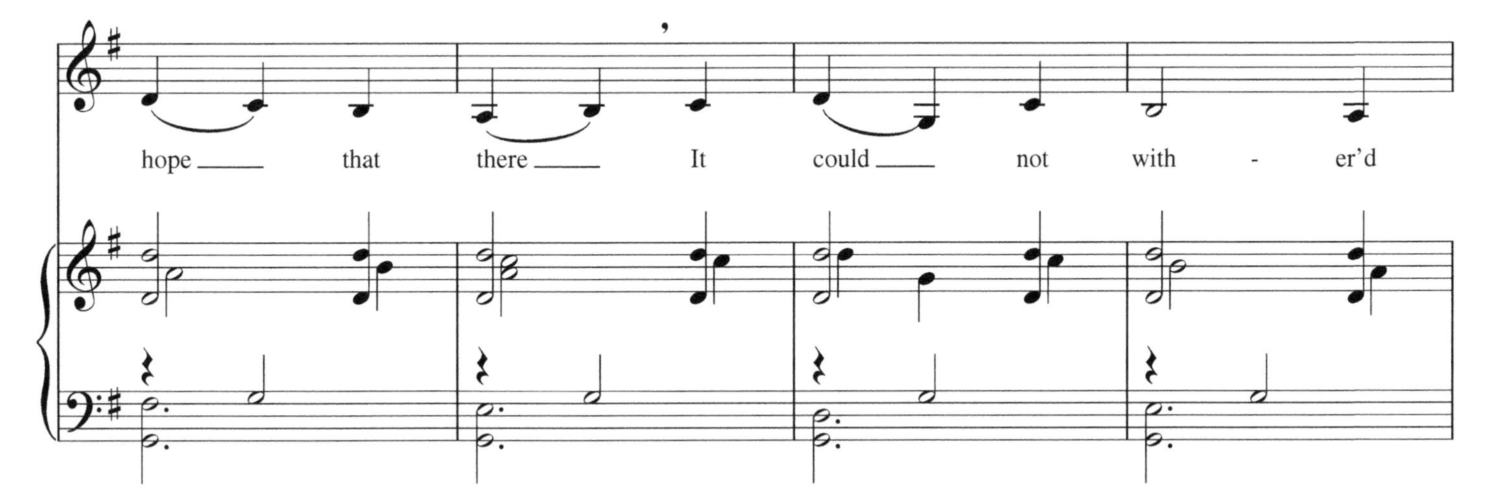
hope that there It could not with - er'd

mf
be; But thou there - on didst

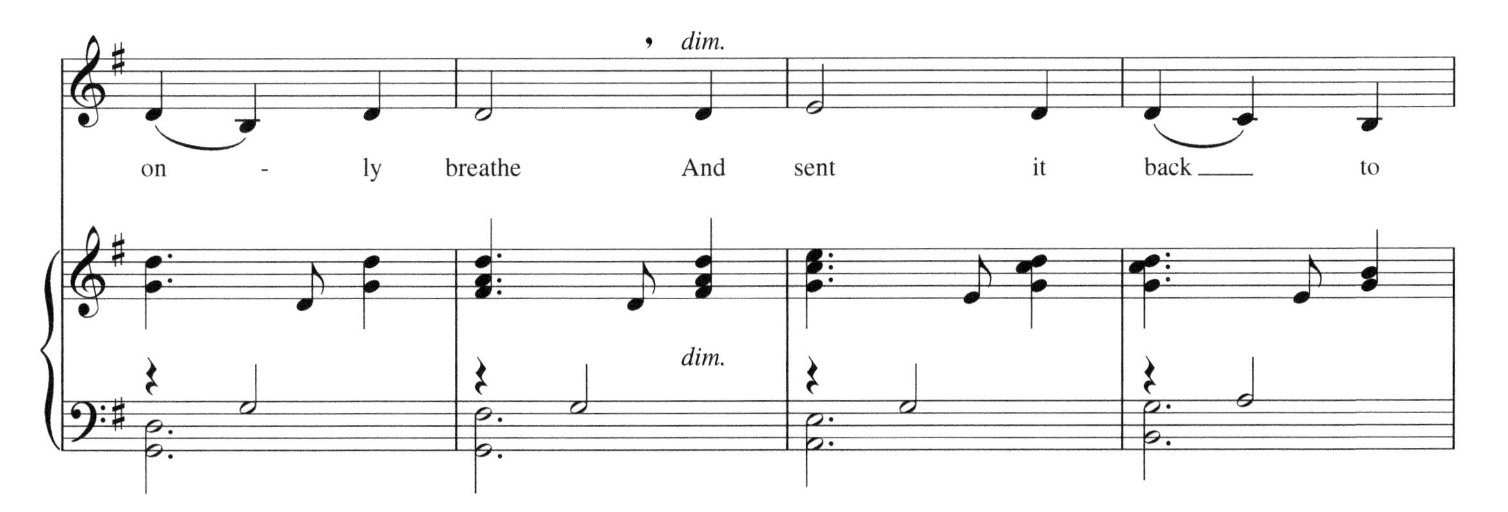
dim.
on - ly breathe And sent it back to

rit.
me,

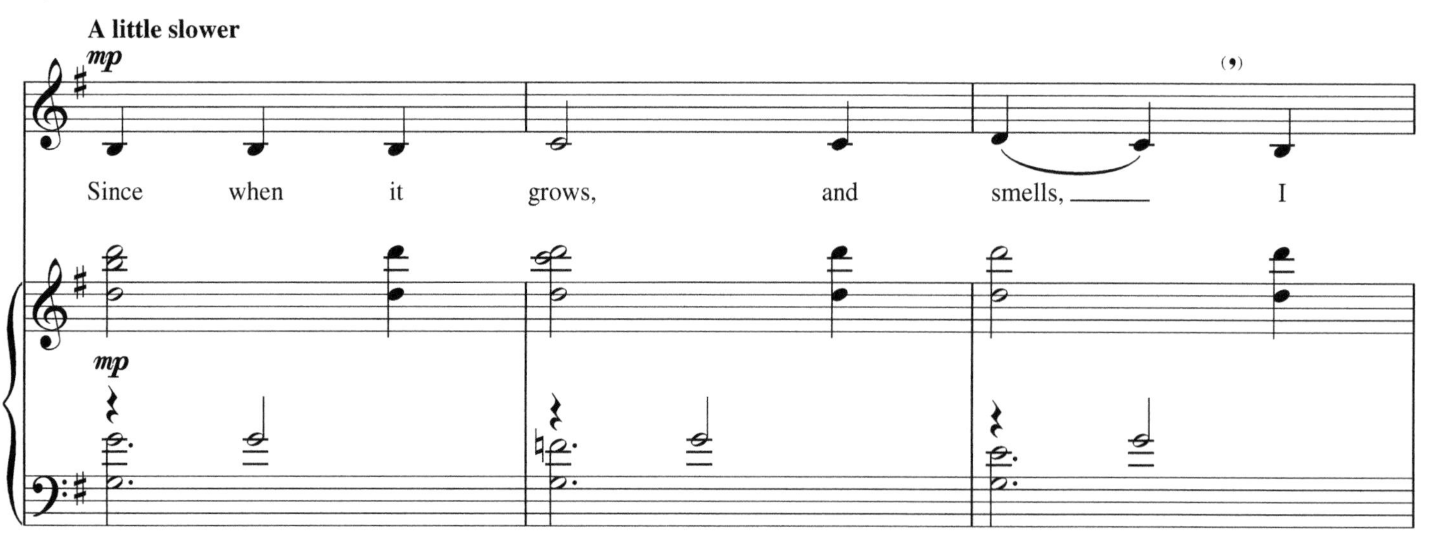
A little slower
mp
Since when it grows, and smells, I
mp

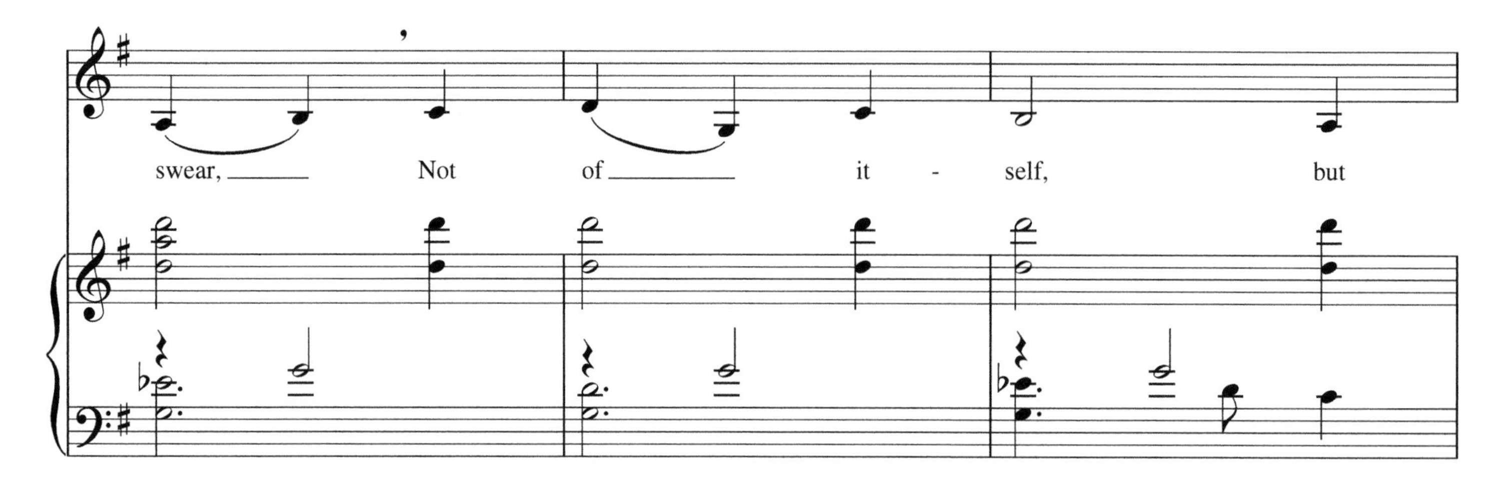
swear, Not of it - self, but

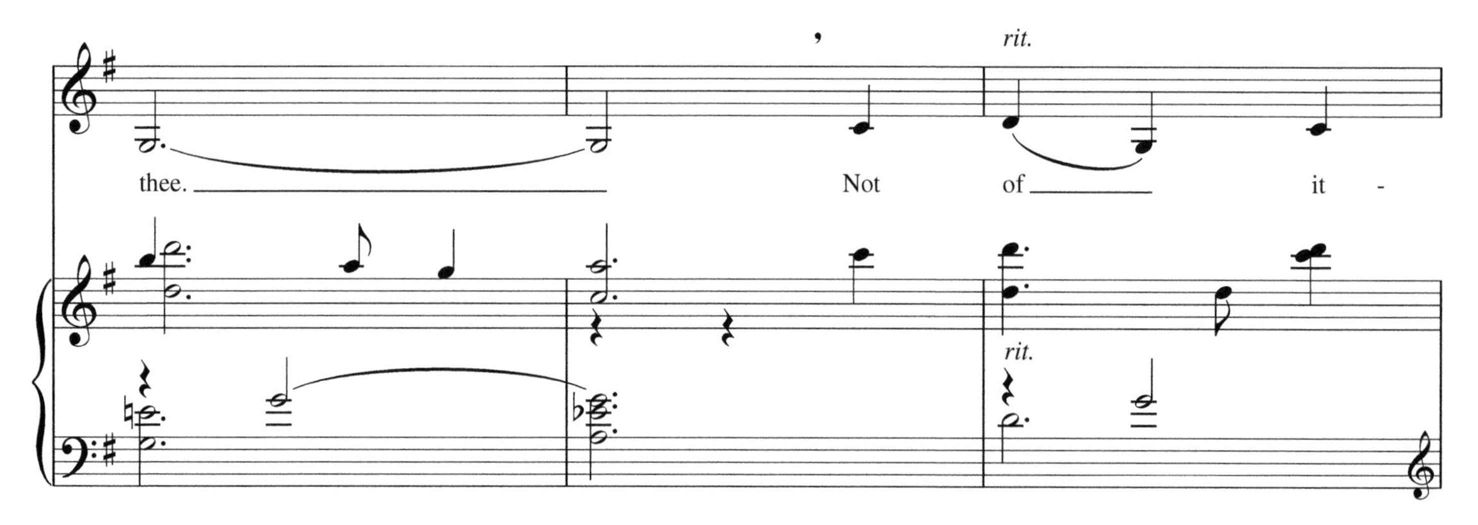
rit.
thee. Not of it -
rit.

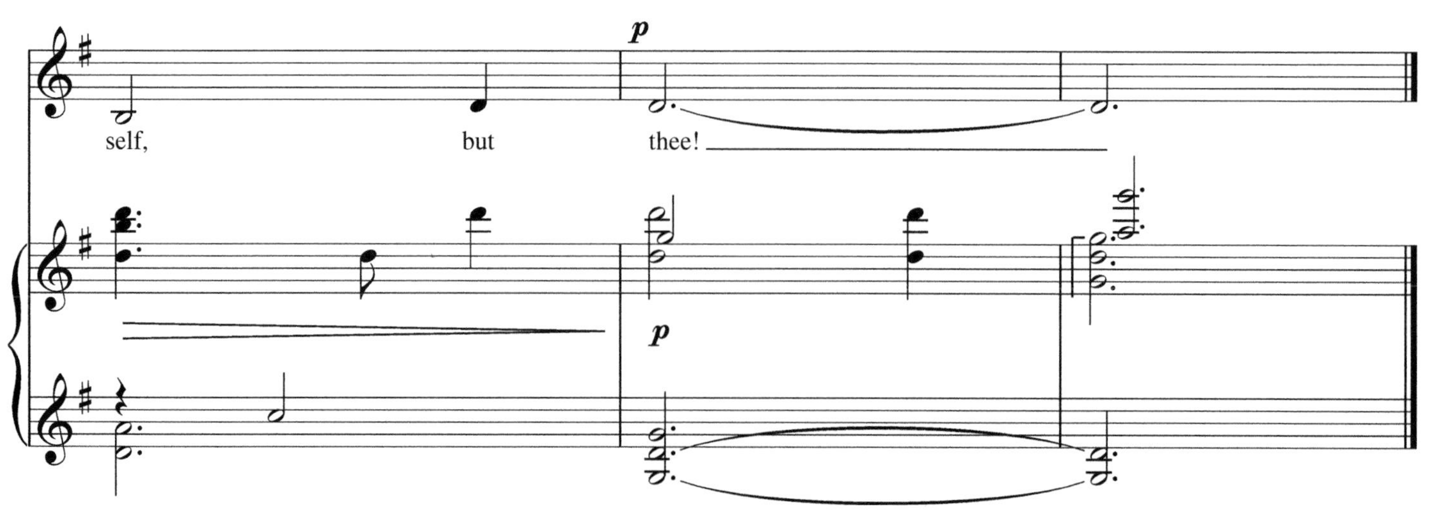
p
self, but thee!
p

It was a lover and his lass

William Shakespeare
(1564–1616)
from *As You Like It*

Thomas Morley
(c. 1557–1602)
realized by Richard Walters

The editors' optional melodic ornamentation is for verse 2, 3 or 4. The singer may choose to sing selected verses.

22
spring! In spring - time,
in spring - time, The

26
on - ly pret - ty ring - time, When birds do sing, hey

30
ding - a - ding - a - ding, hey ding - a - ding - a - ding, hey ding - a - ding - a - ding, Sweet
33
1, 2, 3
4
lov - ers love the spring.
2. Be -
3. This
4. Then,
spring.

The Erie Canal

New York work song, ca. 1820

14
coal and hay, from Buf - fa - lo we're start - ing a trip, and it's a slow _ but a
port of call, a hun - dred friends will greet me "hel - lo," from Al - ba - ny ___ to ___

18
ver - y good ship. Hey!
Buf - fa - lo. Hey!
Low bridge, ev - 'ry - bod - y down! Low bridge, we're a -

22
com - in' to a town! And you'll al - ways know your neigh-bor, you'll al - ways know your pal, If you've

25
1
2
ev - er nav - i - gat - ed on the E - rie Ca - nal! 2. Get E - rie Ca - nal!

I Gave My Love a Cherry

Mountain Song from Kentucky
arranged by Brian Dean

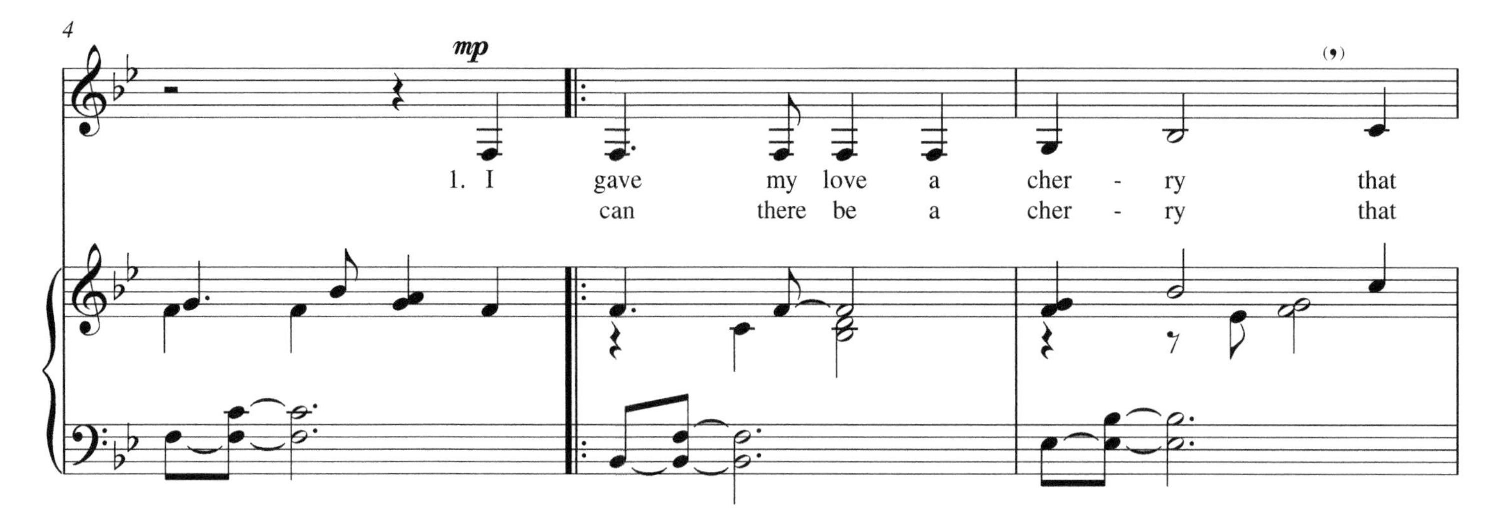

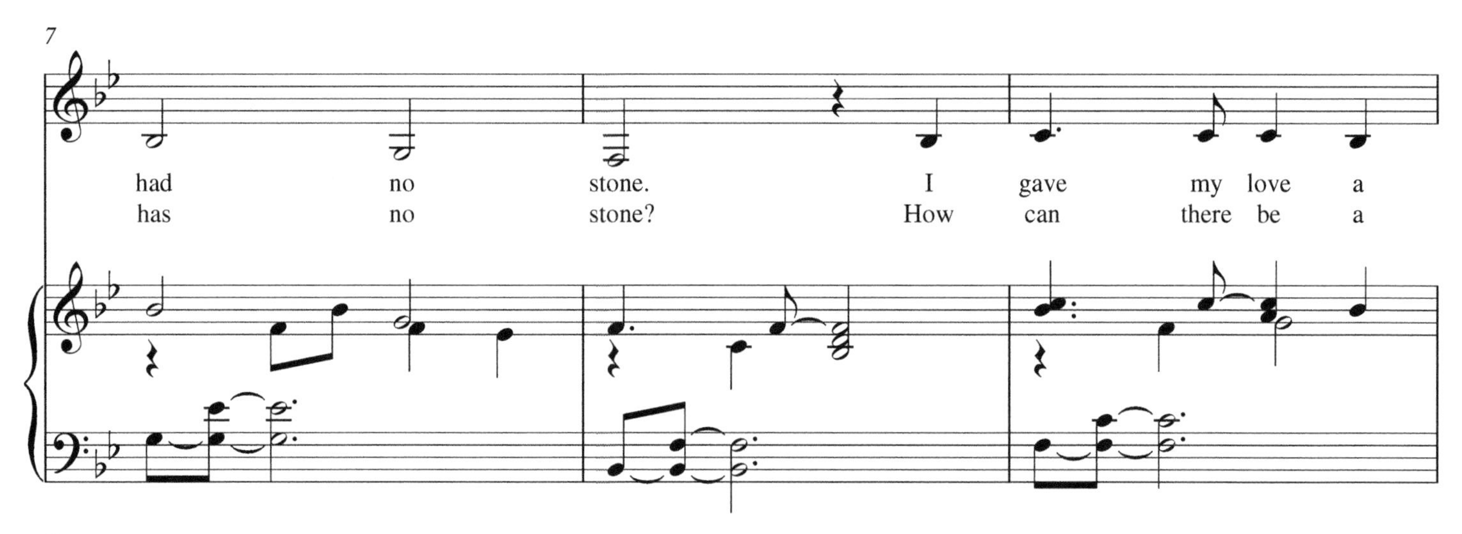

14
sto - ry that has no end. I
sto - ry that has no end? How

17
gave my love a ba - by with no cry -
can there be a ba - by with no cry -

20
1
in'.
23
2
2. How
in'?

26
rit.
p
3. A
rit.

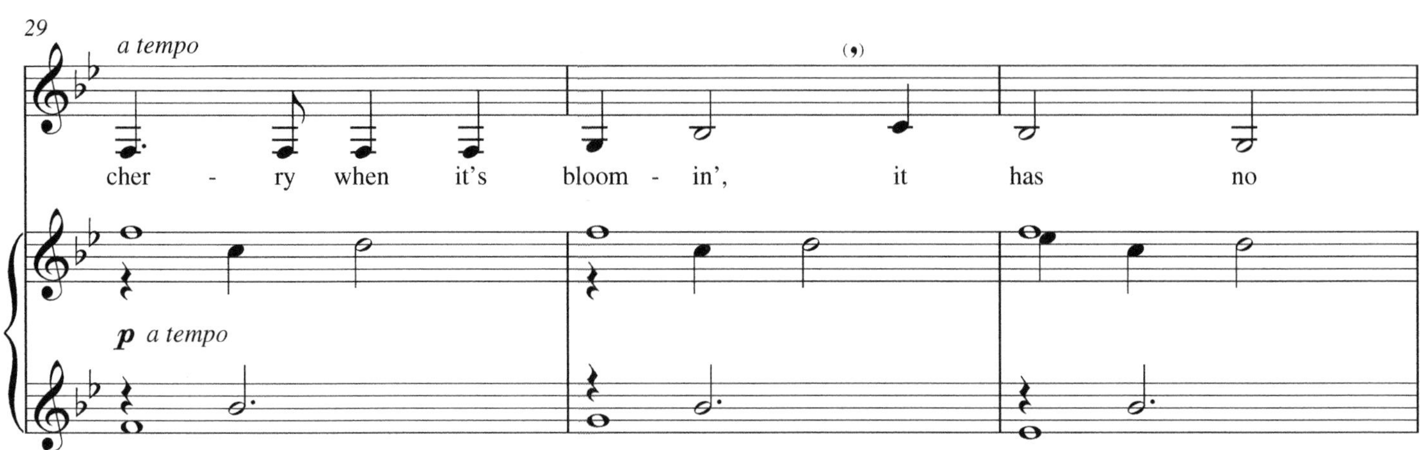
29
a tempo
(,)
cher - ry when it's bloom - in', it has no
p a tempo

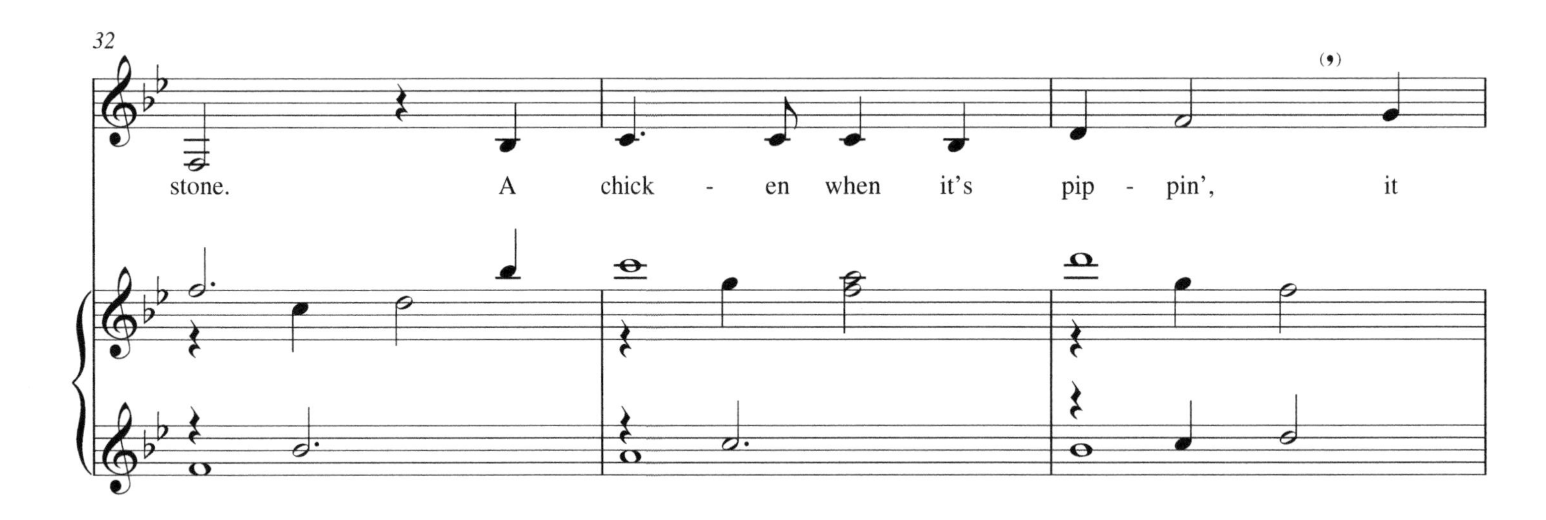
32
(,)
stone. A chick - en when it's pip - pin', it

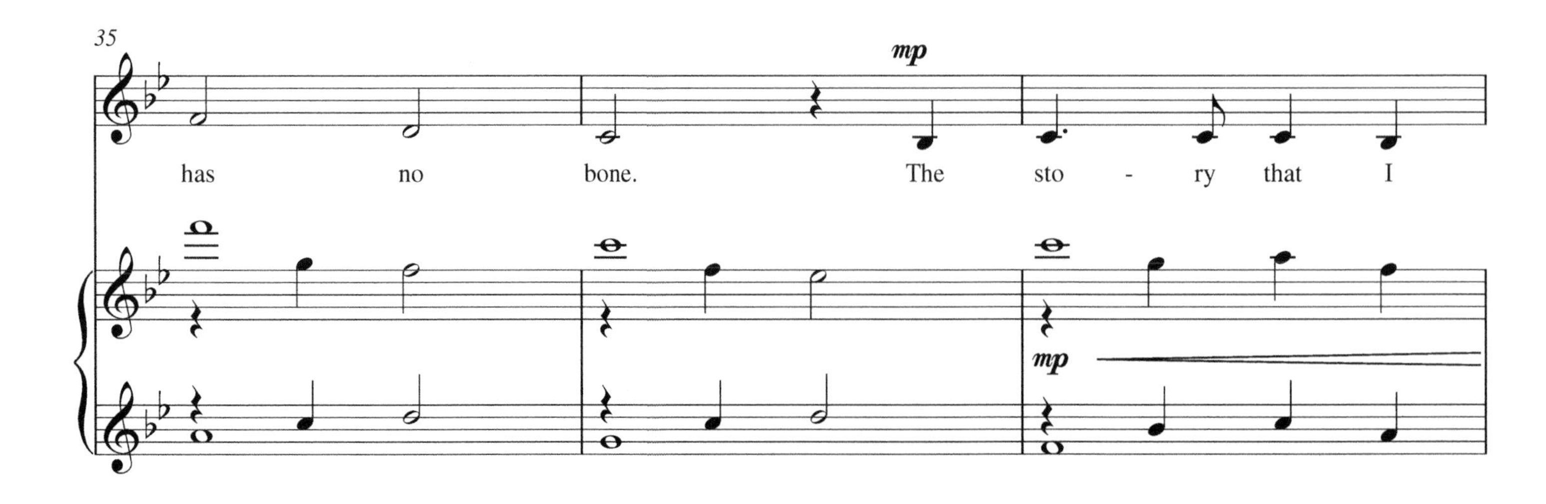
35
mp
has no bone. The sto - ry that I
mp

38
(,)
love you, it has no end.
mf

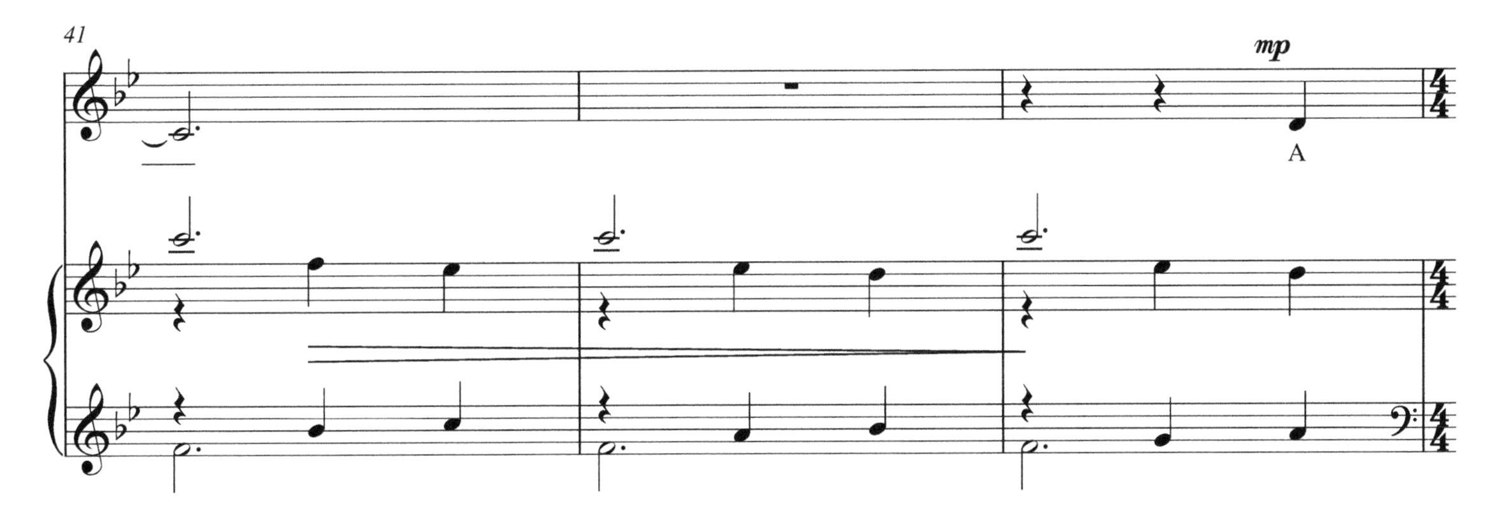
41
mp
A

44
(,)
ba - by when it's sleep - in' makes no
p

47
cry - in'.
pp

The Jolly Miller

English, early 18th century
arranged by Charles Fonteyn Manney
(1872–1951)

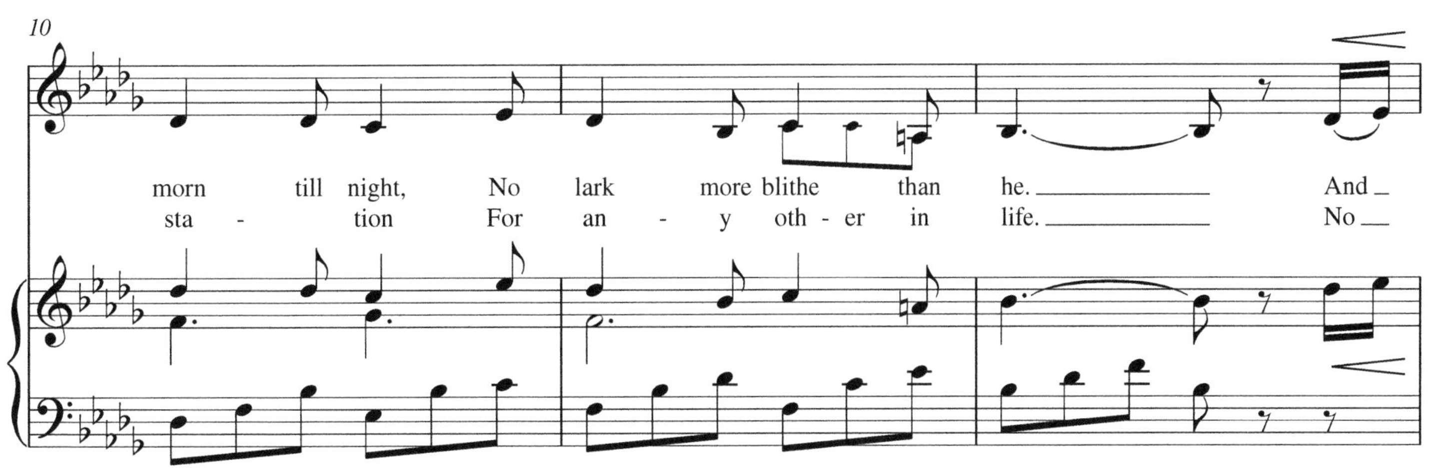
10
morn till night, No lark more blithe than he. And
sta - tion For an - y oth - er in life. No

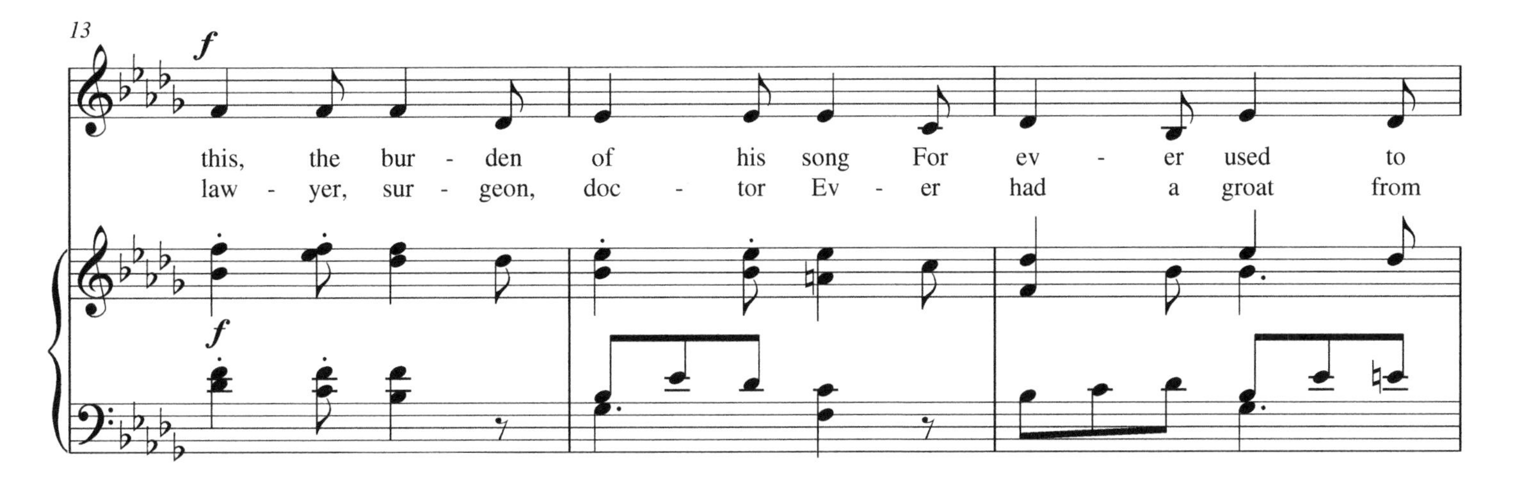
13
f
this, the bur - den of his song For ev - er used to
law - yer, sur - geon, doc - tor Ev - er had a groat from
f

16
be. "I care for no - bod - y, no, not I, And
me, "I care for no - bod - y, no, not I, And

19
1
2
no - bod - y cares for me." 2. I
no - bod - y cares for me."

The Lark in the Morn

English Folksong
Collected and arranged by Cecil J. Sharp
(1859–1924)

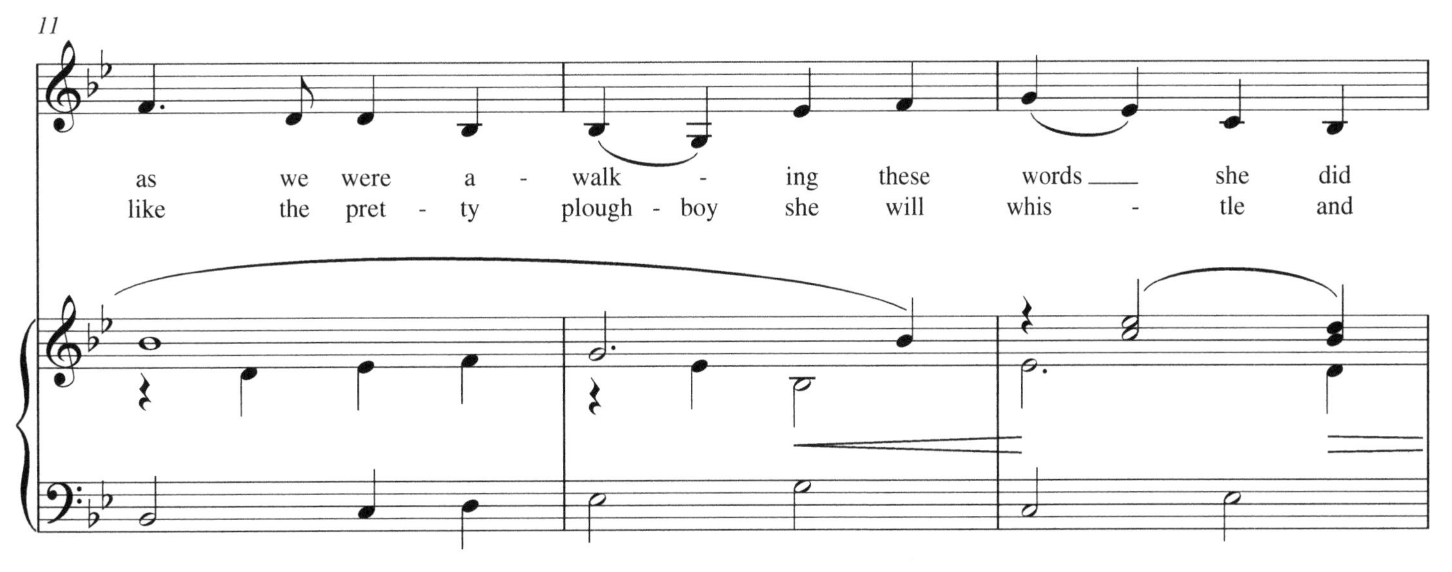
11
as we were a - walk - ing these words ___ she did
like the pret - ty plough - boy she will whis - tle and

14
say: ___ There's no life ___ like a plough - boy's all
sing, ___ And at night ___ she'll re - turn ___ to her
cresc.
dim.

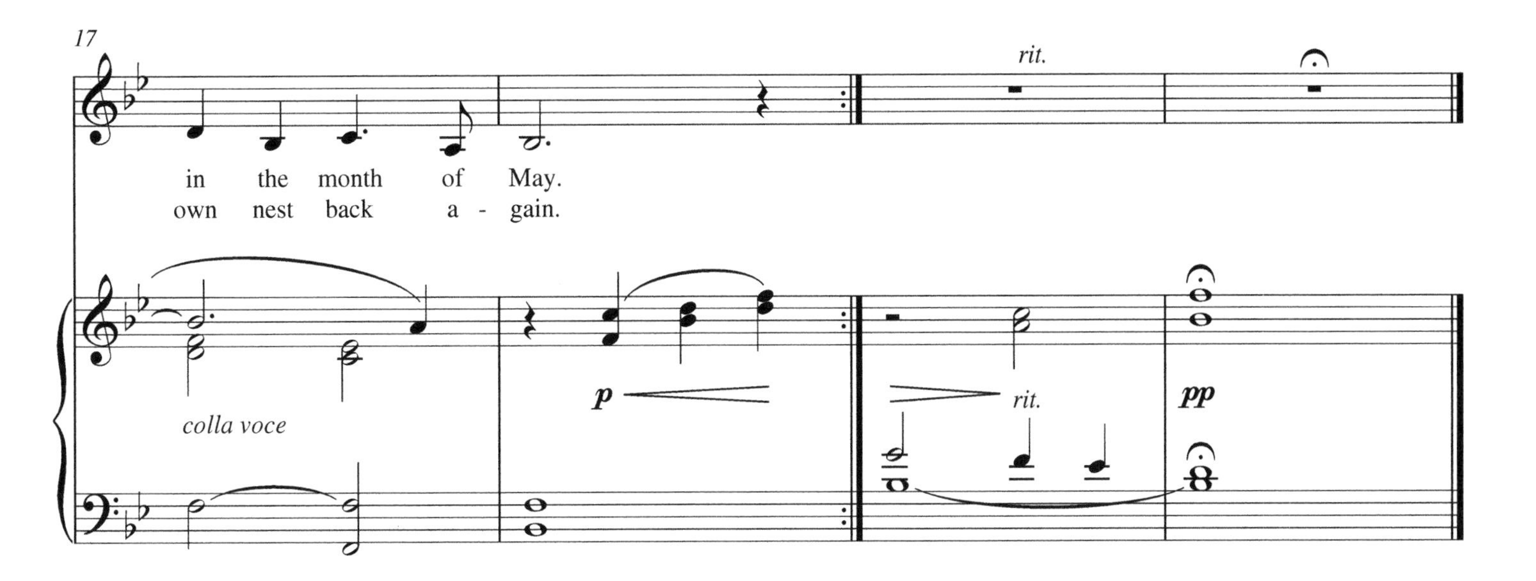
17
rit.
in the month of May.
own nest back a - gain.
colla voce
p
rit.
pp

Pastime with good company

Anonymous, 16th century
attributed to King Henry VIII
realized by Richard Walters

Shenandoah

American Folksong
about the Shenandoah Valley of Virginia

Various versions of this folksong exist, some about an Iroquois chief and his daughter; a later, 19th century sea chantey version was sometimes sung for weighing anchor.

The Rambling Sailor

Collected and arranged by
Cecil J. Sharp
(1859–1924)

12
bid __ you a - dieu, No more to the sea will I go with __ you; I'll
will __ you __ do? Here's ale and __ wine and __ bran - dy __ too; Be -
town __ I ____ went, To court young _ maid - ens __ I was __ bent; And
cresc.
f
dim.

15
trav - el the coun - try __ through and through, And I'll __ be a ram - bling
sides a pair __ of __ new silk shoes, To trav - el with a ram - bling
mar - ry none __ was __ my in - tent, But live __ a ____ ram - bling
mf

18
1, 2
3
sail - or. 2. If
sail - or. 3. The
sail - or.
dim.

The Silver Swan

Orlando Gibbons
(1583–1625)
realized by Richard Walters

15
last, and sang no more.
Fare - well all joys, O

19
death, come close mine eyes.
More geese than swans now live, more fools than

23
wise!
Fare - well all joys, O death, come close mine

27
[rit.]
eyes. More geese than swans now live, more fools than wise!
[rit.]

Simple Gifts

Traditional Shaker Song

10
place just right, 'twill be in the val - ley of

12
love and de - light. When true sim - plic - i - ty is gained, to

15
bow and to bend we won't be a - shamed. To turn, turn will

18
be our de - light till by turn - ing and turn - ing we come out right.

The Streets of Laredo

(Cowboy's Lament)

19th Century American Folksong
based on the Irish Ballad
"A Handful of Laurel"
arranged by Richard Walters

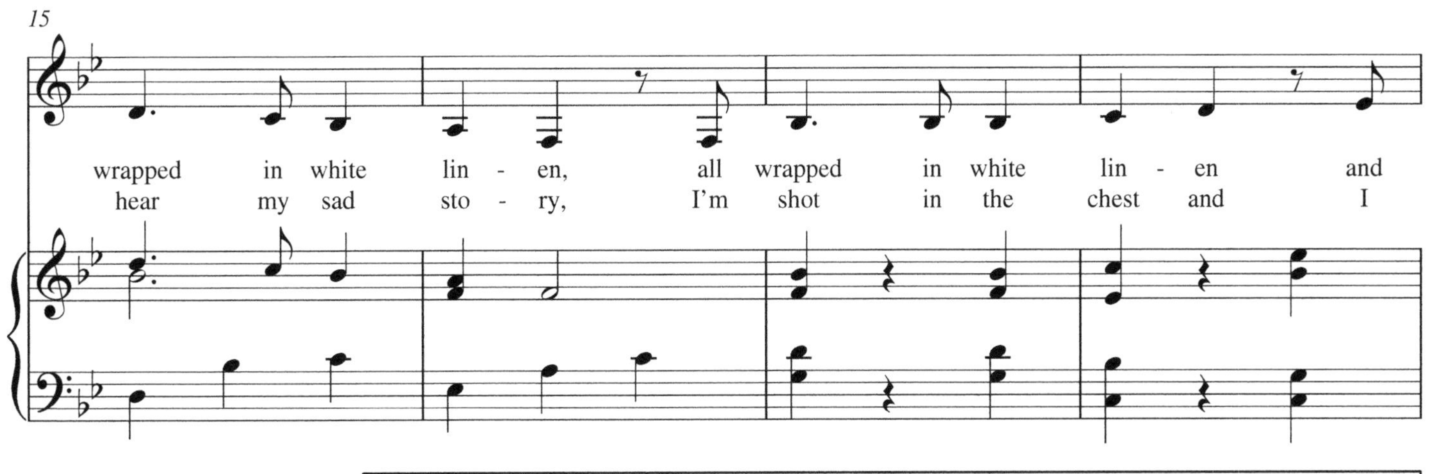
15
wrapped in white lin - en, all wrapped in white lin - en and
hear my sad sto - ry, I'm shot in the chest and I

19
1
cold as the clay.
know I must
2. "I

24
2
die."
3. "It was
mf
mf
p

30
1st time mf
2nd time p
once in the sad - dle I used to go dash - in',
six - teen gam - blers to car - ry my cof - fin,
1st time mf
2nd time p

34
once in the saddle I used to ride away, First
six jolly cowboys to sing me a song. Take
38
down there to Rosie's and then to the card-house. Got shot in the
me to the grave-yard and lay the sod o'er me, for I'm a young
43
chest and I'm dyin' to-day."
cowboy, I know I've done wrong."
1
p
4. "Get
2
49
Slower
p
5. "Oh, bang the drum slowly and play the fife

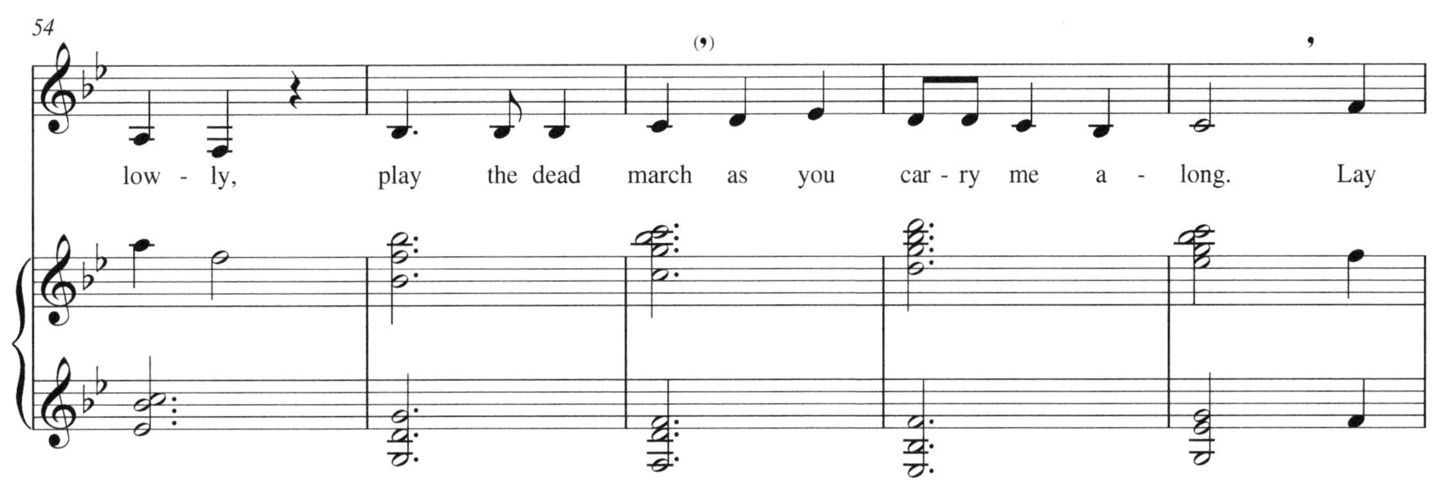
54
(,)
,
low - ly, play the dead march as you car - ry me a - long. Lay

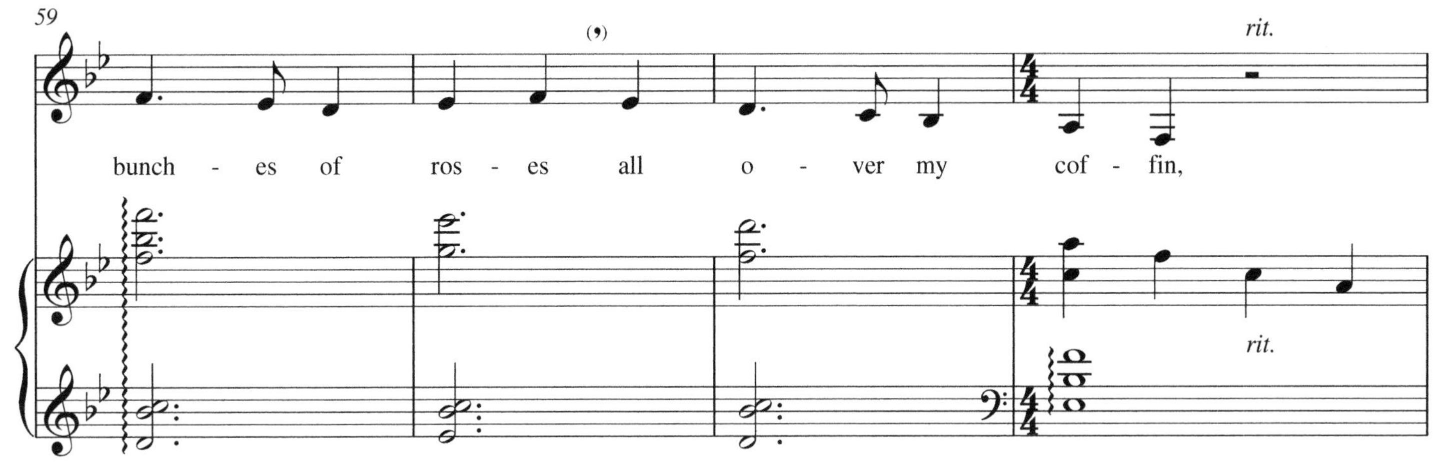
59
(,)
rit.
bunch - es of ros - es all o - ver my cof - fin,
rit.

63
More slowly
rit.
Tempo I
ros - es to dead - en the clods as they fall."
rit.

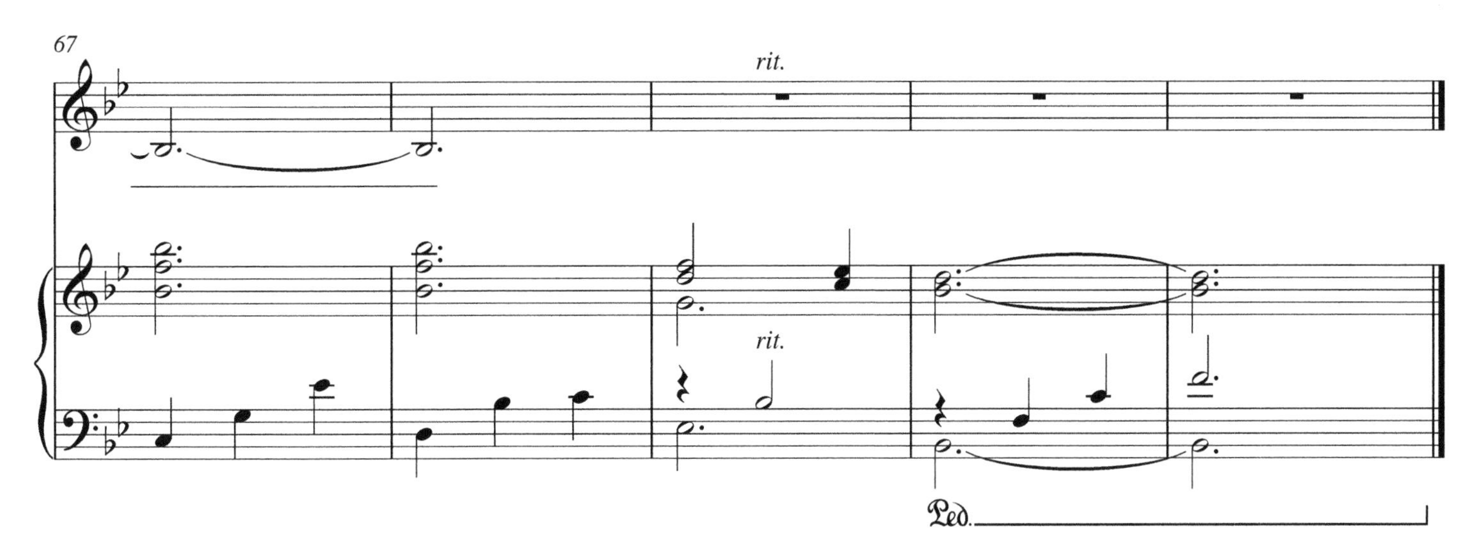
67
rit.
rit.
Ped.

Sometimes I Feel Like a Motherless Child

African-American Spiritual
arranged by Richard Walters

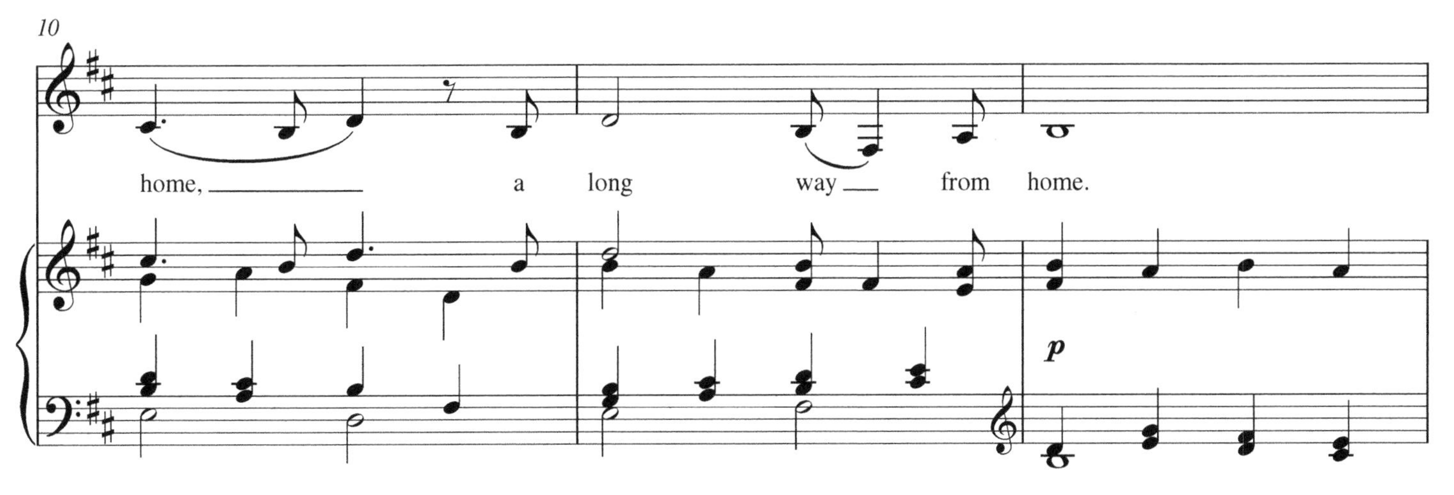
10
home, a long way from home.
p

13
mp
2. Some-times I feel like I'm al - most gone,
mp

16
some - times I feel like I'm al - most gone,

18
some - times I feel like I'm al - most gone, way

20
up in the heav - en - ly land, way

22
mf
up in the heav - en - ly land. Way
24
p
poco rit.
up in the heav - en - ly land, way up in the heav - en - ly
mf
p
poco rit.

27
a tempo
rit.
land.
a tempo
rit.